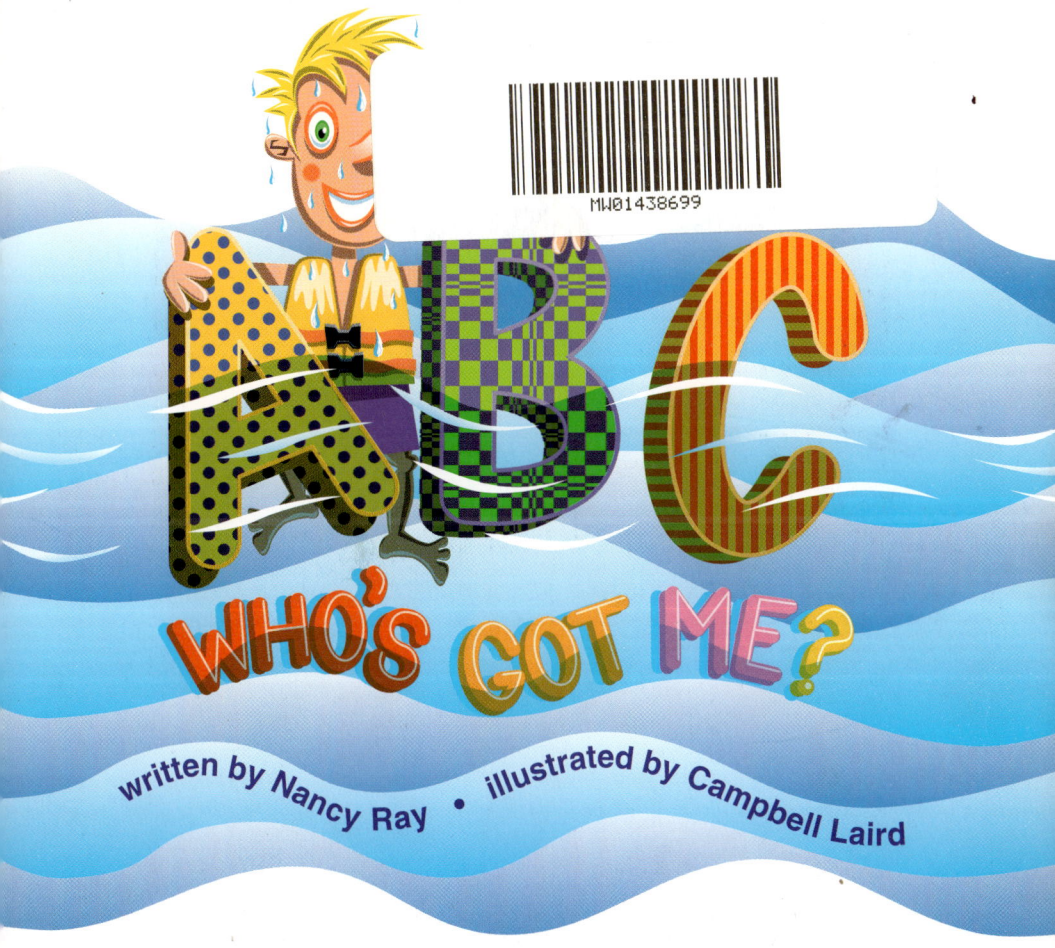

ABC WHO'S GOT ME?

written by Nancy Ray • illustrated by Campbell Laird

HARCOURT BRACE & COMPANY

Orlando Atlanta Austin Boston San Francisco Chicago Dallas New York
Toronto London

A, B, CDE,
Swim, swim in the sea.

F, G, HIJ,
Splash, splash, splash away.

K, L, MNO,
Who has got me by the toe?

P, Q, RST,
I have found a friend for me!

U, V, WXY,
Bye-bye. Do not cry.

And last one is Z.
I will take you home with me.